Dear Parent,

In <u>What Is Electr...</u> ...ur child
will learn about el... ...rons. Dog and
Cat use a set of dominoes to explain
to Christopher how electrons move
quickly from one to another to make
electricity. Then Dog shows Christopher many things that need electricity to work. Find out what they are in
the pages of this book.

Sincerely,

Rita D. Gould

Managing Editor

FAMILY FUN

- Take s...
  with yo...
  outlets...
  electric...
  tion yo...
  ing obj...
  discuss...
  small e...

- Ask you...
  her bed...
  work.

READ M...

- *Why D...*

JUL   1996

This book is a presentation of Weekly Reader
Books. Weekly Reader Books offers book
clubs for children from preschool through high
school. For further information write to:
WEEKLY READER BOOKS, 4343 Equity Drive,
Columbus, Ohio 43228

This edition is published by arrangement
with Checkerboard Press.

Weekly Reader is a federally registered trademark
of Field Publications.

What Is Electricity?

A **Just Ask**™ Book

Hi, my name is Christopher!

by Chris Arvetis
and Carole Palmer

illustrated by
James Buckley

FIELD PUBLICATIONS
MIDDLETOWN, CT.

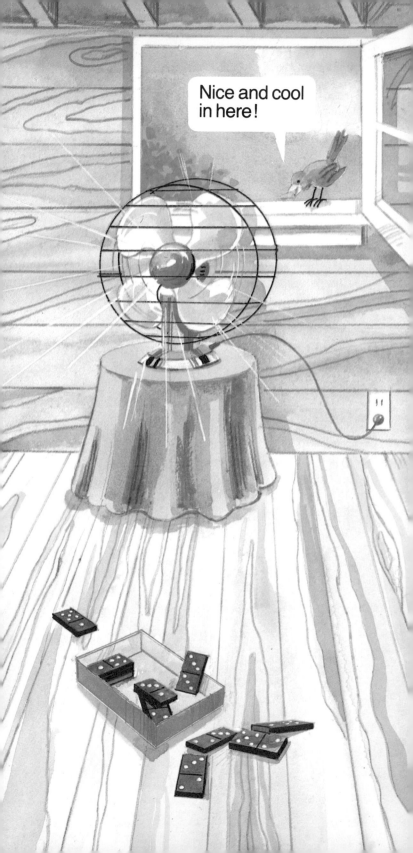

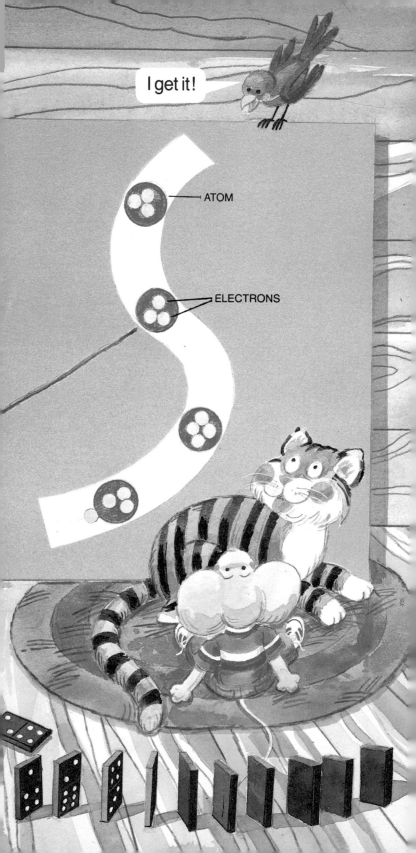

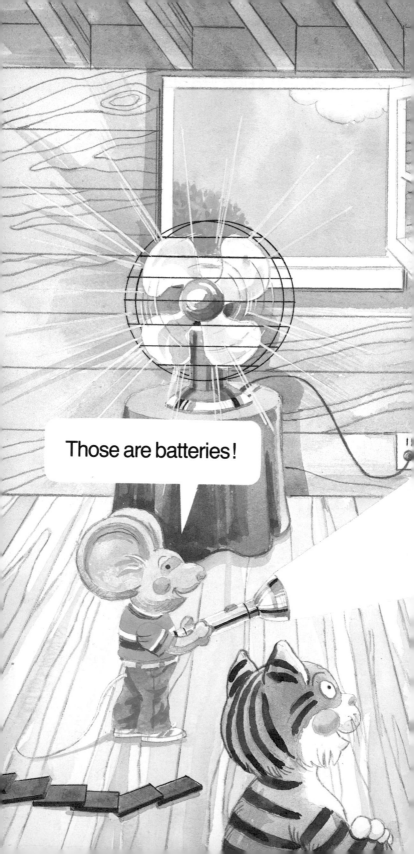

Some people say that electricity works something like the water in a river.

The steady flow of the water keeps the river moving toward a lake or an ocean.

That steady flow is called the current.

Say CUR-RENT.

The current of electricity moves along the wire in the same way.

CUR-RENT!

Let's look around and see what things use electricity.

The stove, the toaster, the mixer, the freezer, and the refrigerator all use electricity.